TURNING POINTS IN HISTORY

Revised and Updated

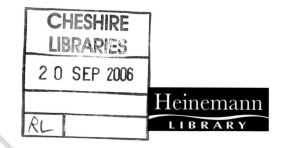
Heinemann
LIBRARY

Pearl Harbor

The US Enters World War II

www.heinemann.co.uk/library
Visit our website to find out more information about **Heinemann Library** books.

To order:
 Phone 44 (0) 1865 888112
 Send a fax to 44 (0) 1865 314091
 Visit the Heinemann Bookshop at www.heinemann.co.uk/library to browse our catalogue and order online.

First published in Great Britain by Heinemann Library,
Halley Court, Jordan Hill, Oxford OX2 8EJ,
part of Harcourt Education.
Heinemann is a registered trademark of Harcourt Education Ltd.

Editorial: Clare Lewis
Designed by Tokay Interactive Ltd.
(www.tokay.co.uk)
Printed in China by WKT Ltd

10 digit ISBN: 0 431 07708 8
13 digit ISBN: 978 0 431 07708 6
10 09 08 07 06
10 9 8 7 6 5 4 3 2 1

British Library Cataloguing in Publication Data
Tames, Richard
Turning Points in History: Pearl Harbor: The US Enters World War II – 2nd edition
940.5'426
A full catalogue record for this book is available from the British Library.

Acknowledgements
The Publishers would like to thank the following for permission to reproduce photographs:
Corbis: pp. **9**, **14**, **17**, **20**, (Bettman) pp. **4**, **13**, **19**, **21**, **23**, (George Hall) p. **28**, (Minnesota History) p. **16**, (Museum of Flight), p. **15**, (The Marineгs Museum), p. **11**; Hulton Getty: pp. **5**, **18**, **24**; Tames, Richard: pp. **6**, **7**, **10**, **25**, **27**; Tony Stone Images: p. **26**.

Cover photograph reproduced with permission of Empics/A P Photo.

The publishers would like to thank Stewart Ross for his help in the preparation of this book.

Every effort has been made to contact copyright holders of any material reproduced in this book. Any omissions will be rectified in subsequent printings if notice is given to the Publisher.

The paper used to print this book comes from sustainable resources.

Contents

Tora! Tora! Tora!   4

Opening up Japan   6

Expanding the United States   8

Pacific rivals   10

A world without work   12

Edging towards world war   14

Hard choices for the United States   16

The great gamble   18

Patriotism and production   20

Victory at sea   22

The United States' Japan   24

Japan's Japan   26

The great debate and Find out more   28

Timeline   30

Glossary   31

Index   32

Some words are shown in bold, **like this**. You can find out
what they mean by looking in the Glossary.

Tora! Tora! Tora!

Total surprise

At dawn on Sunday 7 December 1941 Japanese aircraft launched a surprise attack on Pearl Harbor, the US naval base in Hawaii. Sweeping in from carriers out at sea, they wrecked 21 ships, over 300 planes, and caused 3,500 **casualties**. The Japanese lost just 29 planes, 5 midget submarines, and 64 men. The strike had come without warning, a declaration of war being made only after it had started. To the United States it was not simply **aggression** – it was **treachery**.

Retreat from victory

The Japanese failed to hit three US aircraft carriers out at sea. Not knowing the position of these ships, the Japanese feared a counter-attack. Rather than risk a third attack against Pearl Harbor's oil stores and repair facilities, the Japanese sailed home.

America united

Until Pearl Harbor was attacked many Americans wanted to stay out of the wars raging in Europe and Asia. Pearl Harbor enraged US opinion.

Of the 1,400 crew of the *USS Arizona*, 1,102 were killed. The wreck is now an official war grave. Most of the other ships that were sunk or damaged were repaired to fight again.

Sleeping giant

While his comrades celebrated, Admiral Yamamoto Isoroku, planner of the attack, warned grimly, "I fear we have only awakened a sleeping giant and his reaction will be terrible." Yamamoto, a former naval **attaché** in Washington DC, USA, had opposed war with America.

This newspaper appeared on the Hawaiian island of Oahu, within 90 minutes of Japan's attack on Pearl Harbor. The final death toll was much higher than stated in the headlines.

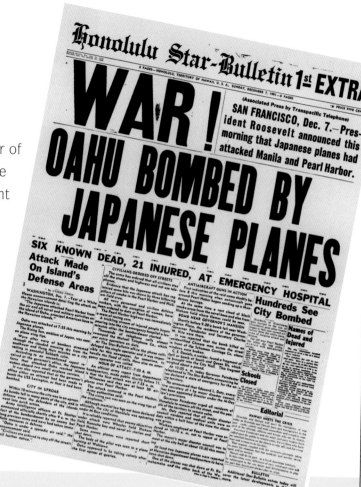

Eyewitness

John Garcia, who was 16 at the time, was a civilian engineer. He remembers the attack and the events that followed.

"I spent the day swimming ... I brought out I don't know how many bodies ... The following morning I went with my tools to the *West Virginia*. It had turned turtle, totally upside down ...

"About 300 men we cut out of there were still alive by the 18th day. It took two weeks to get all the fires out. ... they told me a shell had hit the house of my girl ... they said it was a Japanese bomb. Later we learned it was an American shell. She was killed ... getting ready for church."

President Franklin D. Roosevelt declared to Congress:

"Yesterday, December 7 1941 – a date that will live in **infamy** – the United States of America was suddenly and deliberately attacked by ... the Empire of Japan ... our people, our territory, and our interests are in grave danger ... With confidence in our armed forces ... we will gain the inevitable triumph. So help us God."

Opening up Japan

Japan meets the West – 1

Japan had no contact with western countries until Portuguese ships arrived there in 1543. A century of trade followed, which brought in new technology, such as clocks and guns. From 1639 Japan closed off contact with the outside world, gaining security from intruders but falling behind in technology.

Japan meets the West – 2

War against Mexico (1846–48) brought California under US control. From there Americans wanted to trade with China. In 1853 the US navy forced Japan – at gunpoint – to open up its seaports for US ships to buy food and water, for repair, and for trade. Over the next half century Japan imported western technology and institutions in order to transform itself into a modern industrial and military power.

In 1850 Yokohama was a tiny fishing village of wooden houses. By 1875 it had western-style stone buildings and Japan's first railway.

Enrich the country! Strengthen the army!

Unlike the government of its great neighbour China, which tried to ignore western powers, Japan's leaders saw the West as both a threat and an opportunity. Japan adopted a western-style calendar, coinage, postal system, and weights and measures. German instructors trained the new army. The British built the first railway, trained the navy, and supplied its ships. American advisors reformed education and agriculture. By the 1890s Japan had its own steel mills and shipyards and no longer needed foreign experts. To avoid becoming a **colony** of one of the expanding western **empires**, Japan became powerful enough to create an empire of its own.

The battleship *Mikasa*, the flagship of Admiral Togo during the battle of Tsushima (below). Built in England, the vessel had been launched in 1902.

Japan emerges

Victory over China in 1894–95 brought Japan rice-rich Taiwan as her first colony. In 1902 Britain became Japan's **ally**. This enabled Japan to defeat Russia and gain control of Korea in 1904–05 because Britain kept France, Russia's ally, out of the war. Japanese sea-power was decisive in both these victories. Successful wars made the armed forces popular and powerful in Japan.

The Russo–Japanese war 1904–05

The Russo–Japanese war for Korea began with the Japanese navy trapping the Russian Pacific fleet in its base at Port Arthur in China. On land the two sides fought to a standstill. Meanwhile Russia's Baltic fleet sailed more than half-way round the world to join in. When it reached the Straits of Tsushima in May 1905, Admiral Togo's Japanese fleet conquered the Russian fleet in a matter of hours. After that Russia agreed to peace.

Expanding the United States

From east to west

Colonial America was settled from Europe by sea and prospered by seaborne trade. Quarrels over taxes on that trade led to the war for American independence. That war led to the United States forming its first navy. Americans then spread westward, controlling California by 1849. Now possessing both western and eastern seaboards, they looked to trade with Pacific Asia as well as with Europe.

An admiral's advice

In 1890, US Admiral A.T. Mahan wrote a book called *The Influence of Sea-Power on History*. In it he argued that Britain owed its worldwide empire to its navy. The US navy, important in the American Civil War (1861–65), had been neglected. Mahan recommended that the United States restore its navy, acquire overseas bases, and build a canal through Central America for ships to pass from the Atlantic to the Pacific without going round South America. This would cut the journey from the Caribbean to California by three-quarters, saving 11,250 kilometres (7,000 miles) and six weeks.

The inset location map shows where maps 1 and 2 are. The yellow shows US expansion 1867–1914. Areas too small to show clearly are underlined in yellow. Map 1 – Guam, Wake, Midway, the Hawaiian islands, and Samoa. Map 2 – Panama canal, Puerto Rico, and Guantanamo (Cuba).

US cruisers destroy an outdated Spanish fleet at Manila Bay in the Philippines in 1898.

A new power at sea

The United States listened to Mahan. By 1900 the US navy had grown from twelfth to third largest in the world. US naval power was shown in the Spanish–American war of 1898. At Manila Bay, Commodore Dewey's six modern ships sank ten outdated Spanish ships without losing a single man. Off Cuba, another US fleet lost just one sailor in destroying a second Spanish fleet. This war gave the United States control of the Philippines, Puerto Rico, the Pacific island of Guam, and the right to build a naval base in Cuba. In 1898 the United States also took over Hawaii. In 1908 the US began building a naval base at Pearl Harbor. Between 1907 and 1909 the US navy's "Great White Fleet" of 16 battleships sailed 73,600 kilometres (about 46,000 miles) round the world in a show of strength.

The Panama Canal

Building a canal through Panama started in 1882. It only succeeded after an environmental clean-up of swamps and undergrowth in 1904–06 wiped out mosquitoes carrying **yellow fever** and rats carrying **plague**. The US Corps of Army Engineers completed the 82 kilometre (51 mile)-long canal between 1908 and 1914 for $380,000,000. Thanks to the canal the US Navy could switch its strength quickly to either the Pacific or Atlantic Ocean. The canal is now too small for most modern aircraft carriers.

Pacific rivals

World War 1...

As Britain's ally against Germany in World War I (1914–18), Japan used its navy to capture the German-controlled Shandong area of China and German colonies in the Pacific (the Mariana, Caroline, and Marshall Islands). Japan kept the islands after the war ended in 1918. German U-boat sinkings of **neutral** US ships helped bring the United States into the war in 1917 as one of Britain's allies.

...and after

At the 1919 Paris Peace Conference, US President Woodrow Wilson launched the League of Nations, with the aim of settling disputes between countries peacefully. Unfortunately Wilson, a dying man, could not get the United States itself to join and this weakened the League. The League also refused to adopt a declaration of racial equality suggested by Japan. The Japanese felt that, despite all their efforts to modernize their country, they were still not accepted as equals by Westerners.

The Prince of Wales with Japanese naval officers in 1921. The 20-year-old Anglo-Japanese alliance ended that year. The United States could now fight Japan without coming into conflict with Britain.

The United States and Japan

At the Washington Naval Conference, organized by the United States in 1921–22, Japan was persuaded to agree that, for every five battleships the United States and Britain had, it would have only three. The United States and Britain agreed not to strengthen bases west of Pearl Harbor, giving Japan superiority in its home waters. The Anglo-Japanese **alliance** was dissolved after 20 years. This ended US fears that, in a war with Japan, the United States might risk fighting Britain, too.

In 1924 US Congress passed a law against Japanese **immigration** to the United States. The Japanese took this as a further insult by the West.

The *USS Saratoga* was converted from a battle-cruiser that had been scrapped in accordance with the 1922 Washington Naval Agreement.

The aircraft carrier

Carriers were pioneered during World War I. The first were ordinary warships converted to carry seaplanes. Carriers with flight decks were in service by 1917. Japan's first purpose-built carrier, the *Hosho*, was launched in 1922. Larger ships soon followed. The *USS Lexington* and *Saratoga* and Japanese *Akagi* and *Kaga*, all conversions, were completed in 1927-28. In the 1930s America, Japan, and Britain were the only nations to begin building large purpose-built carriers. The *USS Yorktown* carried 80 planes, the Japanese *Shokaku* 84, *HMS Illustrious* only 55 – but the British design was much better armoured and stronger.

The Americans and Japanese thought carrier-borne planes in large numbers could cripple an enemy fleet at ranges far beyond those of a battleship's guns. World War II was to prove them right and make the battleship **obsolete**. Pearl Harbor was one of the battles to show this.

A world without work

Making jobs

The collapse of world trade between 1929 and 1931 caused mass unemployment in all the industrial nations. Japan was still recovering from a terrible earthquake that had wrecked Tokyo in 1923, killing over 100,000 people. In the United States conditions were made worse by droughts, which turned rich farmlands into "dust bowls". From 1933 onwards President Roosevelt's "New Deal" programme tried to put Americans back to work by funding conservation and building projects. In Germany, Adolf Hitler's **Nazi** government created jobs by building roads and re-arming for a future war.

Making trouble

Japan had few minerals, no oil or rubber and, being very mountainous, had too many farmers for too little land. **Extremists**, especially in the army, favoured expanding the overseas empire by war. This would give Japan access to the raw materials it lacked, markets for its manufacturers, and land on which to settle its growing population. Civilian politicians who said they wanted co-operation with the West rather than war put their lives at risk. When Japan agreed to the London Naval **Treaty** (1930) putting new limits on naval building, Prime Minister Hamaguchi was **assassinated** at Tokyo railway station.

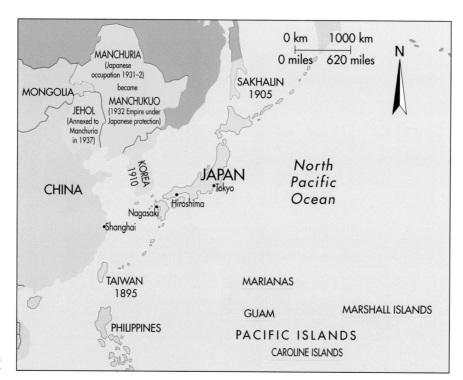

Yellow areas show Japanese expansion in the period 1894–1937. Islands that are too small to be seen are underlined in yellow.

Puyi, the top-hatted puppet ruler of Manchukuo, is surrounded by Japanese generals and officials.

Manchuria becomes Manchukuo

In 1931, without asking permission from the civilian government in Tokyo, Japanese generals ordered troops into the resource-rich Chinese province of Manchuria. In 1932 they set up a **puppet government**, pretending the area was the independent state of Manchukuo. When the League of Nations condemned the invasion as aggression, Japan left the League in 1933. In 1934 Puyi, China's last emperor and a Manchu, was made Emperor of Manchukuo. Real power, however, remained in Japanese hands. In 1937 Japanese troops from Manchukuo began a full-scale invasion of the rest of China.

The 26 February 1936 incident

In 1936 junior army officers used 1,400 troops to seize the Japanese parliament and prime minister's home. They assassinated two ministers and a general and demanded a new government. The rebellion was crushed in days and 19 leaders were shot. However, the army used the uprising to increase its power over government, arguing that this was the only way discontent among junior officers could be controlled. In 1938 a National **Mobilization** Bill geared business up for all-out war production, giving the government strict control over companies, unions, prices, and the media.

Edging towards world war

War in China

By December 1937 Japanese troops had taken Beijing, Shanghai, and Nanjing, where at least 150,000 civilians were massacred. Western eyewitnesses were horrified but helpless. When Japanese planes sank the US gunboat *Panay*, which was carrying Chinese **refugees** near Nanjing, Japan apologized and paid $2,000,000 compensation. The United States accepted this.

Although the United States had accepted Japanese apologies, it wanted Japan to stop the aggression against China. However, US public opinion still favoured staying out of foreign wars and concentrating on getting people back to work after the **Great Depression**. Besides, Japan had an army of 2 million, while the United States' was under 200,000. Although Japanese naval tonnage was only 70 per cent of America's, its carrier tonnage was 94 per cent of the United States'.

A Chinese baby screams amid the wreckage of a Shanghai railway station, bombed by the Japanese.

The United States could hardly threaten war if it was not prepared to re-arm. Japan was divided over the risks of action. A panel of bankers and military advisors reckoned the US economy to be 10 times as productive as Japan's. On the other hand, Japanese generals saw the United States as a country of film stars, gangsters, and jazz, not soldiers. They believed it would protest over China but do nothing.

An American bomber factory – the Japanese greatly underestimated the speed and size of output achieved by US mass-production methods.

Alternative strategies

By 1938 the Japanese army thought its main aim should be to finish conquering China and confront the strong **Soviet** forces on the Manchukuo border. Japan's navy favoured driving into Southeast Asia to get control of supplies vital for domestic industry and overseas warfare: oil, rubber, and minerals such as iron ore. This policy risked war with the British, French, Dutch, and Americans, who all had colonies or interests there.

Defeat and diplomacy

In 1938, and again in 1939, Japanese troops clashed with Soviet forces on the Manchukuo border, leading to large-scale fighting. Soviet armoured units and aircraft beat the Japanese repeatedly, killing over 17,000. The army realized it was not unbeatable and decided to fight on one front at a time. Therefore, in September 1939 the Japanese asked for a ceasefire. The outbreak of war in Europe that month led the **USSR** to agree. In April 1941 the two countries agreed to remain neutral if the other went to war, thus protecting both countries from having to fight on two major fronts.

Hard choices for the United States

Hoping for peace...

When Germany invaded Poland in September 1939, many Americans thought that the United States should stay out of the European war. Opinion in the United States was strongly anti-German, just as it was anti-Japanese over Asia. The Americans hoped Britain and France would be able to resist German aggression and that the the United States would reach a peaceful agreement with Japan over China.

...preparing for war

Germany crushed Poland in weeks, and in the spring of 1940 turned west to conquer the Netherlands, Belgium, and Luxembourg. France **surrendered** in June 1940. Britain **evacuated** its troops, abandoning their equipment. American generals predicted an early invasion of Britain.

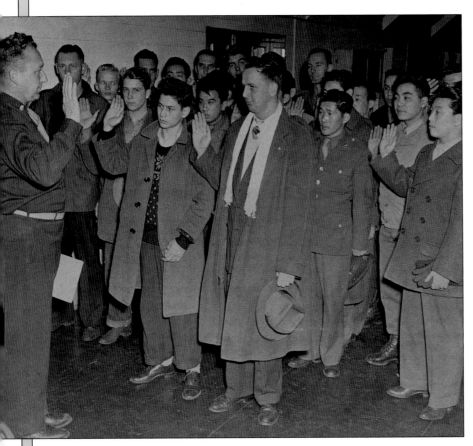

Americans registered in their thousands for military service. These men are enlisting in the army. US pilots, trained in three months, were known as "90-day wonders".

Japan seized the chance to take over France's colonies in Southeast Asia. As the situation worsened in both Asia and Europe, US defence efforts expanded rapidly. In September 1940 – for the first time in its history – the United States ordered men to register for possible military service. By December 1941, US army and airforce manpower had risen to 1.6 million and the number of navy vessels from 1,100 to 1,900.

US support

Roosevelt believed that, despite defeats, both Britain and China would continue resistance and that US security would be best served by supporting them without actually going to war.

Roosevelt pledged that the United States would be the "**arsenal** of **democracy**" – supplying the weapons Britain and its allies needed to defeat the dictatorships of Hitler (in Germany) and Mussolini (in Italy). This meant sending supplies to Britain and having the US navy escort the ships carrying them, even at the risk of fighting German U-boats. In China it meant supporting anti-Japanese resistance with supplies and volunteer pilots. Meanwhile, the United States banned the export of oil and scrap metal to Japan.

The Flying Tigers

The Flying Tigers were formed in April 1941 by Claire L. Chennault, a retired US Army Air Corps officer and training expert. He recruited 100 pilots and 200 ground crew to help China against invading Japanese forces. They trained at a British base in Burma and defended the Chinese city of Kunming and the "Burma Road" supply route that carried supplies to Chinese troops. The Flying Tigers destroyed 286 Japanese aircraft for the loss of 50 US aircraft and nine pilots.

The Flying Tigers' proper name was the American Volunteer Group, but the origin of their nickname is obvious.

The great gamble

Planning for a knock-out

Faced with the United States' rapid arms build-up, Japanese leaders decided the United States meant war after all. They thought Japan's best chance of victory lay in destroying the US Pacific fleet at Pearl Harbor. They believed the United States would then be unable to act to prevent the conquest of Asia for at least 18 months. By then Japan's new empire would be secure behind the world's biggest ocean.

As war was unavoidable, Japanese planners wanted to start before the United States got even stronger. While Japan negotiated in Washington, Admiral Yamamoto planned his surprise attack on Pearl Harbor.

Pearl Harbor – mistaking the dangers

US forces realized an enemy first strike was possible, but expected it would be at the Philippines, only 320 kilometres (200 miles) from Japanese-controlled Taiwan. In the remote Pacific island of Hawaii, where 150,000 local people – 37 per cent of the population – were of Japanese descent, the main fear was of **sabotage**.

An aerial view shows how Pearl Harbor's "Battleship Row" made an ideal target.

Looking the wrong way

Planes were therefore lined up close together to make it easier to guard them – this also made them an easier target for enemy planes. Any attack on Hawaii was expected from the Japanese-controlled Marshall Islands, 3,200 kilometres (2,000 miles) to the southwest. No long-range air **reconnaissance** was ordered, and on the morning of Sunday 7 December 1941 most anti-aircraft guns were unmanned and without ready supplies of ammunition.

Swiftly, silently...

Yamamoto's plan depended on sailing six carriers and their support ships from Japan across 5,500 kilometres (3,400 miles) of the Pacific without being spotted. Keeping radio silence – and shielded by bad weather – the Japanese **task force** managed to sail within 450 kilometres (280 miles) of Pearl Harbor undetected and then launch its attack from the north.

A furious President Roosevelt asks Congress to declare war on Japan. The United States did so on 8 December 1941.

A diplomatic disaster

Japanese **negotiations** continued in Washington to the very last. On Saturday 6 December there was a staff send-off party at the Japanese embassy. As a result of heavy drinking, only two senior staff were on duty next morning when the coded message came from Tokyo carrying a formal declaration of war. Without junior staff, who were much faster at decoding and typing, the two officials failed to hand the declaration over to US officials until half an hour after the attack on Pearl Harbor had started, instead of 30 minutes before, as intended. Americans were predictably outraged.

Patriotism and production

Relocation

In 1941 there were 120,000 people of Japanese descent (*Nisei*), two-thirds of them US citizens, living on America's west coast. This was where a Japanese invasion was thought most likely. Without much evidence to back it up, Japanese-Americans were suspected of disloyalty to their adopted country. So, 112,000 *Nisei* were forced to leave their homes and businesses and live in 10 camps in inland states such as Arizona, Colorado, Wyoming, and Arkansas.

Despite this treatment, over a thousand imprisoned *Nisei* volunteered to serve in the US armed forces. No Japanese-Americans were proved to have taken part in spying or sabotage. In 1944 the US Supreme Court ruled that relocation was **unconstitutional** and the camps were closed. Between 1948 and 1965 Japanese-Americans were paid $38,000,000 to cover their losses – less than a tenth of their value. Fewer than 10,000 Americans of German or Italian descent were relocated in this manner.

Proving a point

To prove their loyalty to the USA, thousands of Japanese-Americans volunteered. A Japanese-American unit, the 100th Battalion, composed largely of Japanese-Americans born in Hawaii, won so many medals for being wounded in action that it became known as "the Purple Heart Battalion". It later became part of the 442nd Regimental Combat team, which was the most decorated in US military history, winning four Distinguished Unit Citations in North Africa, France, and Italy. In 225 days of combat the 10,000 men who served in it won 18,143 individual decorations.

On the way to an unknown destination – relocated Japanese-Americans wait at a reception camp.

Collecting scrap rubber for the US war effort – rubber was one of the few key resources that the United States could not produce itself.

Arsenal of democracy

Japanese planners estimated that the United States could produce 10 times as much as Japan. They were wrong; in fact it produced even more. As America geared up for war, its vast natural resources and skilled labour force enabled it to feed and arm 12 million men and women, as well as helping it to support its allies overseas. In 1940 Roosevelt's promise to build 50,000 planes was met with amazement; by 1945 300,000 had been built.

The US Army Air Force had 2,470 planes in 1939. By 1944 it had 79,908. In addition, US shipyards turned out 147 carriers and 215 submarines, 952 other warships, 5,200 merchant ships, and 88,000 landing craft. The US Navy expanded twentyfold to become the biggest in the world.

The USA also produced two-thirds of the world's oil supplies. A tenth of all US food production went abroad, mostly to the USSR and to Britain, where it supplied the millions of US soldiers ready for the invasion of Europe.

Victory at sea

After inflicting huge damage on the US Pacific fleet at Pearl Harbor, the Japanese captured many Pacific islands. They intended to keep the **Allied Powers** at arm's length, to prevent the bombing of Japan and any interference in their Asian conquests. As America and its allies fought to roll back Japanese advances, four great naval battles were fought.

Battle of the Coral Sea, 4–8 May 1942

Coral Sea was the first battle in history when opposing fleets never saw each other. Both relied on carrier-based planes as their main weapon. Japan aimed to take Port Moresby, New Guinea, as its base for invading Australia. Because Allied code-breakers read Japan's naval orders, the US navy knew the Japanese plans. The United States suffered heavier losses, but Port Moresby was saved.

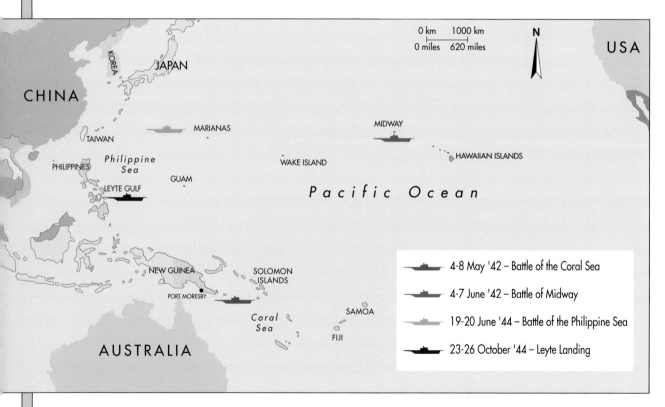

4-8 May '42 – Battle of the Coral Sea
4-7 June '42 – Battle of Midway
19-20 June '44 – Battle of the Philippine Sea
23-26 October '44 – Leyte Landing

Major aircraft carrier battles of the Pacific war 1942–44.

Battle of Midway, 4–7 June 1942

The Japanese sent 145 ships to take Midway island, hoping to force the United States to defend it. From Midway they intended to take Hawaii. The United States once again decoded Japanese messages, so US Admiral Nimitz could plan accordingly. The Japanese lost four aircraft carriers, a blow from which they never recovered. From Midway onwards they could no longer go on the offensive.

A *kamikaze* attack – most *kamikaze* planes were destroyed well before hitting their targets.

Battle of the Philippine Sea, 19–20 June 1944

The largest carrier battle of the war took place while US troops were fighting for the Mariana islands, from where Japan could be bombed. Against a much stronger American fleet, the Japanese lost 3 more carriers, 17 submarines, and almost 400 planes – over 90 per cent of their remaining carrier-based aircraft.

Battle of Leyte Gulf, 23–26 October 1944

Japan's attempt to prevent US forces from recapturing the Philippines led to the biggest naval battle in history. The Japanese had changed their code so this time the US fleet did not know of their enemy's intentions. Nevertheless, in a series of actions US airpower proved decisive. The Japanese lost four carriers and left the US navy undisputed master of the Pacific.

Kamikaze

In 1281 and 1284 the Mongol rulers of China sent huge fleets to invade Japan, but they were destroyed by typhoons, which the Japanese called "*kamikaze*" (divine wind). As the war turned disastrously against Japan in 1944, suicide squads were formed to crash their planes on invading ships. Known as *kamikaze* pilots, they sank a US escort carrier at Leyte. When US forces invaded Okinawa, 2,000 *kamikaze* pilots sank 36 ships and damaged 368 more. By the war's end some 5,000 *kamikaze* had died.

The United States' Japan

The United States advances

US forces bypassed the islands where Japanese forces were strongest. As Japan lost its naval power, these islands could no longer be reinforced or supplied. The first Japanese-held island to be taken, between August 1942 and February 1943, was Guadalcanal in the Solomon islands. The Japanese managed to evacuate 13,000 troops, abandoning their sick and wounded. Guadalcanal cost around 1,700 US lives and at least 17,000 Japanese lives. In June 1944 US forces took Saipan in the Marianas, from where they could bomb Japan itself. US forces had planned to take Saipan in three days. It took three weeks.

Paying the price

In February 1945, after 72 days of bombing, 110,000 Americans landed on Iwo Jima, an island half-way between Saipan and Japan. They had hoped to take the island in 14 days – it took 36. Japanese commanders knew they could not win the war but hoped high losses would make the Allies negotiate for peace, rather than demand Japan's complete surrender. On Okinawa the 172,000 US troops suffered 50,000 casualties. The Japanese lost 110,000 soldiers, plus 150,000 civilians.

Lt General Richard K. Sutherland (left) accepts Japan's surrender, aboard *USS Missouri*, 2 September 1945.

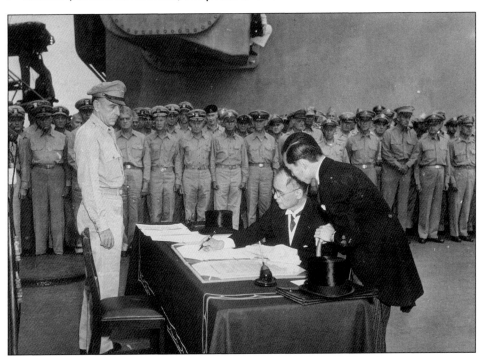

The end – destruction

In March 1945 US bombers killed 100,000 civilians in a three-day raid on Tokyo. By May, 13 million Japanese were homeless. In August the dropping of atomic bombs on Hiroshima and Nagasaki and the USSR's invasion of Manchukuo finally forced Japan to surrender.

A new beginning – democracy

For the first time in its history Japan had been invaded by foreign forces. Under Allied **occupation** Japan adopted a **democratic** constitution that guaranteed citizens' rights and gave women the vote. Land was given to peasant farmers. Independent **trade unions**, mass media, and political parties were allowed. Education was reformed.

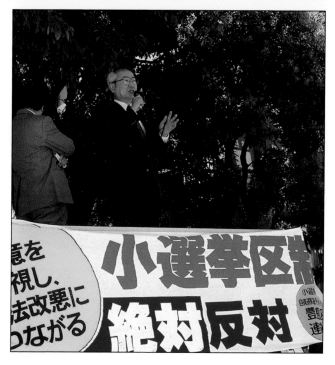

Japan's democracy is now more than half a century old. Here, politicians try to catch the voters' interest on the streets at the 1993 elections.

The popular conqueror

General Douglas MacArthur (1880–1964) graduated from West Point military academy with the highest ever marks. In 1905 he went to Tokyo as assistant to his father, a general. Douglas MacArthur ended World War I as a general himself, with 13 decorations for bravery. In the 1930s he organized the Philippine army. In 1942 he lost the Philippines to the Japanese, only to reconquer the islands in 1945. As Supreme Commander of the Allied Powers, MacArthur took charge of the occupation of Japan. A strong supporter of democratic reforms, he became very popular with the Japanese. In 1950 he became Commander-in-Chief of UN forces against **communist** aggression in Korea and organized a daring and successful landing behind enemy lines. When he called for the bombing of communist China, President Truman dismissed him for trying to interfere in a political – rather than military – decision.

Japan's Japan

Wealth...

The occupation of Japan ended in 1952. Some US troops remained because Japan and the United States had become allies. The new constitution drawn up by the Allied Powers for Japan only allowed small forces for self-defence, so it could spend more on building new industries. In 1958 Japan launched the world's largest oil tanker. By 1964 it was wealthy enough to host the Olympics. It started the world's first "bullet-train" service and soon became the world's biggest producer of ships, cars, cameras, radios, and television sets.

Later Japan switched away from heavy goods, such as steel and chemicals. These caused pollution and needed large imports of energy and raw materials which Japan did not have. Instead it used its highly educated workers to make computers, photocopiers, and other advanced "light" goods. By 1990 Japan had seven times as many industrial robots as the United States, and the world's largest merchant fleet.

The 200 kilometres (124 miles) per hour bullet train is a symbol of Japan's post-war revival.

...and health

The Japanese became not only richer than ever before but healthier too. By 2000 life expectancy in Japan was 77 years for men and 83 years for women, compared with 73 and 80 in the United States. The United States has more doctors per person than Japan but spends just over one and a half times as much on health as on defence. Japan spends almost five times as much on health as on defence.

Japan in the world

Japan joined the United Nations in 1956 and remained a close ally of the United States. By the 21st century it was second only to the United States in giving aid to poor countries and paying for the United Nations.

In the 1970s Japanese companies began building factories in Southeast Asia, Europe, and North America. By 1992 Japan had invested $386 billion abroad, almost half of it in the United States. The number of Japanese working or studying abroad had grown to 680,000.

Although this development made Japan an economic superpower, it was still not willing or able to use military might overseas. During the 1990–1991 Gulf War, for example, it took no part in the fighting but paid $13 billion towards the cost of liberating Kuwait. It also gave $110 million to help Kurdish refugees and sent pollution experts to help clean up damaged oilfields. In 1992 Japan changed its laws to allow up to 2,000 troops to serve abroad on peaceful UN missions.

Diggers made at the Komatsu factory in northeast England, the area which has the largest concentration of Japanese investment in Europe.

The great debate

The rights and wrongs of Japan's surprise attack on Pearl Harbor have been hotly debated. So too is today's position of the United States as the world's policeman.

Question 1: The attack on Pearl Harbor, was it both criminal and foolish?

Yes!

- Although war is brutal, there are internationally accepted rules to help protect the innocent. An undeclared attack breaks these rules.
- The US government had done its best to avoid war with Japan, trying diplomacy and economic sanctions instead.
- The US public did not want war before Pearl Harbor.
- Large-scale modern wars are won by industrial power – Japan should have realised it could not hope ever to defeat the United States in the long run.
- If the Japanese had studied the US way of thinking they would have realised that a sneak attack was the surest way of turning the entire nation against them.

No!

- Feeling that war with the United States was inevitable, was it not just common sense for the Japanese to strike the first blow?
- War is about life and death; it is foolish to think of it as a sport governed by rules of fair play.
- Japan and the United States were of such unequal strength that if the Japanese had waited until the US was ready for war they would have been at an even greater disadvantage.
- The United States was partly to blame for Pearl Harbor by forcing Japan into a corner with economic sanctions.
- Some believe in the "conspiracy theory" that the US government secretly wanted the Japanese attack in order to get public opinion on the side of war.

What do you think?

The United States now has troops and hi-tech aircraft carriers stationed around the world to take action in loca trouble spots. Japan's forces are much more limited.

The world's policeman.

Victory in World War II left the United States and the communist USSR as the world's only superpowers. Between 1947 and 1985 there was dangerous rivalry between them that at times came close to sparking a Third World War. In the end, though, the cost of competing with the United States ruined the Soviet economy and the USSR collapsed. This left the US as the only superpower, a world policeman with troops and bases all round the world.

Question 2: Does it matter if the United States is the only superpower?

Yes!

- If it wishes, the United States can act almost alone – as it did when it invaded Iraq in 2003.
- Although the United States is a democracy, real power rests with its super-rich businesses.
- There is no guarantee that a US president, commander of its armed forces, will act responsibly.
- US economic power is stronger but less obvious than its military power.

No!

- The democratic United States sets an example of freedom to all
- The United States cannot act entirely alone. It has to listen to the European Union, Russia, and China.
- The United States generally behaves responsibly, supporting freedom and good government everywhere.
- The United States usually acts through the United Nations.

What do you think?

Find out more

Using the Internet

Explore the Internet to find out more about the attack on Pearl Harbor and World War II. You can use a search engine, such as www.yahooligans.com or www.google.com, and type in keywords or phrases such as *Great Depression*, *kamikaze*, *Battle of Midway*, *North Atlantic Treaty Organization*, or *Hiroshima*.

More books to read

Aki Becker, Michelle. *World Tour: Japan*. (Raintree, 2004)
Connolly, Sean. *Witness to History: World War II*. (Heinemann Library, 2003)
Ross Stewart. *Causes and Consequences of the Second World War*. (Evans Publishing Group, 2003)
Tames, Richard. *Turning Points in History: Hiroshima: the Shadow of the Bomb*. (Heinemann Library, 2006)

Timeline

1543		First Europeans land in Japan
1639		Japan cuts off foreign trade
1853		USA forces Japan to re-open foreign trade
1868		Japan's new government begins modernizing reforms
1890		A.T. Mahan publishes *The Influence of Sea-Power on History*
1894–5		Japan defeats China and takes over Taiwan
1902		Anglo–Japanese alliance
1905		Japan defeats Russia
1904–14		Panama Canal built
1910		Japan takes over Korea
1914–18		World War I
1917		USA enters World War I
1919		League of Nations founded at Paris Peace Conference
1922		Washington Naval Conference limits naval building
1924		USA bans immigration by Japanese
1929		World trade collapses
1930		London Naval Treaty limits naval building
1931		Japan takes over Manchuria
1932		Manchukuo established
1933		Japan leaves the League of Nations
1937		Japan attempts to conquer all China
1939		Outbreak of World War II in Europe
1940		Japan takes over French colonies in Southeast Asia
1941	7 December	Japan attacks US naval base at Pearl Harbor, Hawaii
1942	February	Japan captures Singapore, Britain's main military base in East Asia
	4–8 May	Battle of the Coral Sea
	4–7 June	Japanese navy defeated at Battle of Midway
1943	February	USA takes Guadalcanal
1944	19–20 June	Battle of the Philippine Sea, Saipan taken
	23–26 October	Battle of Leyte Gulf
1945	March	US bombers devastate Tokyo
	April	US forces invade Okinawa
	6 August	Atom bomb dropped on Hiroshima
	8 August	USSR declares war on Japan
	9 August	Atom bomb dropped on Nagasaki
	14 August	Japan surrenders
	28 August	US troops land in Japan
1946		Japan adopts a democratic constitution
1949		North Atlantic Treaty Organization founded
1950–53		Korean War
1951		Peace treaty signed between Japan and the United States
1964		Japan hosts Olympic Games
1970		Japan installs first industrial robots
1989		Death of Emperor Hirohito
1998		Japan hosts Winter Olympic Games in Nagano

Glossary

aggression	unprovoked attack
alliance	partnership of friendly nations
Allied Powers	countries fighting together against Germany, Italy, and Japan in World War II, also known as the Allies
ally	a nation or state that is friendly to another nation
arsenal	place for storing or making weapons
assassinate	murder, usually for a political reason
attaché	literally "attached", a diplomat with special expert knowledge
casualties	people killed or wounded
colony	land ruled by a foreign government
communist	follower of communism
democracy	system of government based on the equal right of all citizens to choose and change their leaders freely
diplomacy	relations between nations conducted by peaceful means
empire	group of countries ruled by another
evacuate	take to safety
extremist	someone with such strong views they are not prepared to give way at all
Great Depression	period after the financial panic and collapse of world trade in 1929; the worst was over by 1933
immigration	movement of people into a country
infamy	evil reputation
mobilization	organization of people or resources for war
Nazi	National Socialists Workers Party in Hitler's Germany
negotiations	settle a problem or dispute by talking and compromise
neutral	on nobody's side
obsolete	completely out of date
occupation	rule by a foreign army
plague	disease carried by fleas, often on rats, and often fatal
puppet government	government that makes no real decisions but is ruled by another authority
reconnaissance	survey of an area to locate the enemy or strategic features
refugees	people forced to move from their normal home
sabotage	deliberate damage to stop something working properly
Soviet	belonging to the Soviet Union
surrender	give in, admit defeat
task force	armed force organized for a particular operation
trade union	organization to protect rights and interests of workers
treachery	betrayal by deception
treaty	official agreement between different countries
unconstitutional	against the laws protecting basic rights
USSR	Union of Soviet Socialist Republics; an empire in which communist Russia controlled neighbouring countries from 1917 to 1991; also known as the Soviet Union
yellow fever	acute tropical disease that attacks the liver, heart, and kidneys; often fatal.

Index

aircraft carriers 4, 11
American Civil War
    (1861–65) 8
Anglo-Japanese alliance 10,
    11, 30
atomic bombs 25, 30

Britain 7, 10, 11, 16, 17

China 7, 10, 13, 14, 16, 17,
    25, 30
colonies 7, 8, 10, 15, 16
communism 25
Coral Sea, battle of the 22,
    30

Flying Tigers 17
France 7, 16

Germany 10, 12, 16
Great Depression 12, 14
Guadalcanal 24, 30
Gulf War (1990–91) 27

Hiroshima 25, 30

Iwo Jima 24

Japan 6–7, 17
    Allied occupation 25, 26
    allies 7, 10, 26, 27
    army 14, 15
    attack on Pearl Harbor 4,
        5, 18–19, 30
    economic superpower 26,
        27
    expansionism 7, 10, 12,
        15, 16
    gears up for war 12, 13, 14
    global investment 27
    invasion of China 13, 14
    invasion of Manchuria 13
    naval battles 7, 22–3
    navy 10, 11, 14, 15
    re-opens to foreign trade
        6, 30
    social and political reforms
        25
    surrender 24, 25, 30
    in World War I 10

kamikaze 23
Korea 7, 25, 30

League of Nations 10, 13, 30
Leyte Gulf, battle of 23, 30
London Naval Treaty (1930)
    12, 30

MacArthur, General Douglas
    25
Mahan, A.T. 8, 9, 30
Manchukuo (Manchuria) 13,
    15, 25, 30
Midway, battle of 23, 30

Nagasaki 25, 30
naval battles 7, 9, 22–3
New Deal programme 12
Nisei 20
North Atlantic Treaty
    Organisation (NATO) 30

Okinawa 24, 30

Panama Canal 8, 9, 30
Paris Peace Conference
    (1919) 10, 30
Pearl Harbor 4–5, 9, 18–19,
    30
Philippine Sea, battle of the
    23, 30
Poland, invasion of 16
Port Moresby 22

Roosevelt, Franklin D. 4–5,
    17, 19, 21
Russia 7
Russo-Japanese war (1904–5)
    7, 30

sabotage 18, 20
Saipan 24
Singapore 30
Soviet Union 15, 30
Spanish-American war (1898)
    9
Taiwan 30
Tokyo 12, 30
Tsushima, battle of 7

United Nations 27

United States 22–3, 26
    anti-communism 29
    arms build-up 16, 18
    army and air force 14, 16,
        21
    enters World War I 10, 30
    enters World War II 19
    expansionism 8, 9
    foreign policy 28–9
    Great Depression 12, 14
    immigration laws 11, 30
    Japanese-Americans 20
    military actions since 1945
        28, 29
    military service 16, 20
    naval battles 22–3
    navy 8, 9, 11, 14, 16, 17,
        21
    war effort 15, 16, 21
USS Arizona 4

Vietnam War (1964–73) 29

Washington Naval
    Conference (1921–22) 11,
    30
Wilson, Woodrow 10
World War I (1914–18) 10,
    30
World War II (1939–45) 11,
    15, 16–17, 19, 22–5, 30

Yokohama 6